No Greater Love

Bl. Gianna Beretta Molla

Heroic Witness to Life

By Ann M. Brown

*Blessed Gianna with her
husband and children*

Prologue

Monday, April 30, 1962, 3 p.m. The place: the town of Magenta, near Milan, Italy.

An air of quiet grief pervades the countryside which has recently come back to life in the spring weather. The houses and shops of the town are practically emptied of their inhabitants. They have all gone to pay their respects, to say their final good-byes, to their dearly beloved doctor, Gianna Beretta Molla, who died this past Saturday. She was not even forty.

Her small children, not quite understanding what is happening, walk with their broken-hearted father behind the coffin as they accompany Gianna to the cemetery. Pierluigi, the oldest at five years old, tugs at his father's hand, pointing to the coffin, "Why is mamma closed in that box? Where is mamma going?" Later, he tells his father, "There must be a little house of gold for mamma."

Pietro, though too grief-stricken at that moment to respond to his little son, agrees. Later on, he commissions a gold mosaic to adorn the walls surrounding his wife's burial place. In the burial chapel, one can see the Latin words *Fidelis usque ad mortem,* "Faithful unto death," adorned with a cross and olive branches.

Who was this woman, Gianna, so beloved by so many?

A Wedding Card

The year was 1908. A young bride, recently married in Milan, Italy, sat looking over the wedding cards and gifts she had received. One of the cards caught her eye. It featured a cartoon of thirteen smiling children gathered in a pot. Without hesitation, Maria de Micheli Beretta exclaimed enthusiastically, "All!" as if to say, "I choose them all, I want them all!"

Maria and her new husband, Alberto Beretta, felt that "children are a gift from the Lord," as the Psalmist says. They prayed earnestly that their love would be fruitful. Oddly enough, the wedding card proved to be somewhat prophetic. Thirteen children were born to the Berettas, eight of whom survived infancy. The second youngest, Gianna, was born on October 4th, 1922.

The Beretta parents were Third Order Franciscans, and, though they were not oppressed by poverty, they taught their children to live in great simplicity, frugality, and joy. One of their sons, later a priest, says that they "lived an intense life of piety and evangelical mortification, renouncing even exteriorly all that was superfluous." Gianna, who was later to become a model mother herself, learned self-sacrifice and heroism from her own mother. Maria's cousin recalls: ". . . [A]s the mother of thirteen children, she attended to each one as if she had only that one. She considered the education of her children almost a fulfillment of the work of God in His creatures, almost the creation of souls, a divine undertaking, a priesthood." This cousin further said of Maria that, ". . .hardworking and always very busy, [she] did not neglect missionary work which she held very dear." These very same attributes would be noted in the life of her daughter Gianna.

Both parents attended Mass with their children very early every morning in the nearby parish church, and the Rosary was recited together in the home each evening. After the Rosary, the family repeated the consecration to the Sacred Heart and other prayers. Then they would relax together; the children would play the piano and spend the evening in happy conversation with their parents, while the mother sewed and crocheted lace for altar cloths.

The youngest daughter, Virginia, later related: "Never did a strong or uncontrolled word disturb the serenity of the family, never was a reproof from the mother without the support of the father or vice versa; always in accord and always unswerving, they loved their children and desired to give them a sound and complete formation. The atmosphere of the home was permeated with serenity and peace," while, she adds, necessary punishments and corrections were never neglected.

Their parish priest remembered: "I always saw the parents serene and smiling; in the most painful events of their life, as in the sickness and death of their children, I saw them as serene martyrs of the will of God, though they had agony and death in their hearts. The great solicitude of Papa Beretta was always to keep the children attached to the family and far from occasions of sin. Honesty in his office work was scrupulous."

The parents made sure that each of the children studied a profession so that he or she would be able to carry out, in some way, Christian service to the community and permeate the professional world with the example of a Christian life.

From such a faith-filled seedbed as this, who could doubt that great things would come? Indeed, the eldest daughter, Amalia, died a saintly death in her 20's; Ferdinando became a respected doctor; Francesco became a civil engineer; Enrico, the next son, studied medicine and then became a Capuchin priest, dedicating himself to the missions in Brazil; Zita studied pharmacology; Giuseppe also studied engineering and became a diocesan priest; Gianna, with whom we are concerning ourselves here, became a doctor and died in a heroic act of self-sacrifice; and Virginia, the youngest, became a doctor and a Canossian Sister, working as a missionary in India.

Gianna's Childhood

One may have the impression, at this point, that Gianna was simply a haloed heroine. However, though living in the serenely devout atmosphere of her family, she was a very normal child. Virginia later related that Gianna was "always ready to do all she could for her little sister. . . directing her towards good, putting up with her little tantrums, and sharing in her games." She noted further: "Incidents were not wanting in which both were punished together. . . Gianna consoled her little sister taking her in her own bed, or making her laugh and play. . . . Their cheerfulness sometimes surpassed the limits to such an extent that the punishment, far from being what it was meant to be, became an occasion of great freedom to indulge in other pranks. . . ." It is also related that Gianna was not always ready to obey her mother when called.

However, she always showed herself much inclined towards goodness. When the other children sometimes wished to play pranks which were not altogether in good taste, Gianna reacted immediately and firmly: "No, no, this is a sin!"

Due to the careful training by her parents and oldest sister, Gianna was allowed to make her First Communion at the age of five and a half. From then on, she went to Mass and received Communion daily, whatever the weather or the state of her studies. It was only when, as a mother, she had to feed and prepare her children for nursery school at the same time as Mass that she had to give up this daily banquet, which sacrifice truly cost her.

School Days

The same year in which she made her First Communion, little Gianna started school. Skipping down the street with her ABC book in her bag, she began the long years of studies which would culminate in her earning a medical degree. Like many other children, however, Gianna was not very eager for school. She preferred playing at home with her many brothers and sisters to any class, however lively.

The parents wished to give all their children the best possible human and Christian formation as a solid foundation for life. Therefore, they entrusted their sons and daughters to Catholic schools staffed by teaching Sisters.

Gianna was not a brilliant student. She struggled with her studies, especially as she reached the upper elementary grades and high school. Even in religion, which she enjoyed, she barely passed. At times she had to repeat subjects, and thus, to her great chagrin, missed out on part of the family summer vacation. On one such occasion she wrote, complaining, to her sister Zita, "I have nothing else to do but to study, and. . . Amen! I am here alone, no playing!"

Her letters written to her parents and siblings at those times show much affection for her family, but also display many grammar and spelling mistakes. Gianna was a lover of nature, and she preferred outdoor activity to studying.

In 1933, the Beretta parents celebrated their twenty-fifth wedding anniversary, surrounded by their eight living children. On this occasion a family portrait was taken, and in it we can see Gianna, who was eleven, with her serious, innocent, dark eyes.

One of her teachers around that time paints a picture for us of her impressions of Gianna:

"She was a dear child who knew how to arouse the sympathy and affection of those who approached her due to the simplicity and sweetness of her character and the exquisite sensitivity of her innocent soul, candid like a flower which has blossomed in spring in the warm and serene intimacy of her family. Her face was always smiling, though it was sometimes veiled with a slight melancholy which called for tenderness. I tried to read in her deep and meek eyes the thoughts that in those brief moments disturbed her heart, but I never dared to violate the secret of her intimacy. . . I never heard a word of annoyance, fatigue or rebellion cross her lips. . . . The fulfillment of her duty at home, in school, in society were for her a sacred duty."

One of her school companions wrote later that "Gianna had a faith so catching that all those who met her, after a short time, felt attracted to the Church, in whose life we desired to participate with deeper religiosity." Thus the power of her example made itself felt from her early years.

The Beretta family in 1933 on the 25th anniversary of the parents. Front row, left to right: Gianna, Mrs. Beretta, Virginia, Amalia, Mr. Beretta, Giuseppe. Back row: Francesco, Ferdinando, Zita, Alberto.

A Turning Point

When she was fifteen years old, a great sorrow befell Gianna's family. Her dearly loved oldest sister, Amalia, who had never enjoyed very good health, died an edifying death at the age of twenty-six.

After this, Papa Beretta moved the family to Genoa so that his sons and daughters could more easily continue their studies. That spring, Gianna made a retreat, which, it seems, sparked a change in her priorities. Already used to making a daily meditation, Gianna began to take her duties and her studies more seriously. We still have her resolutions from that retreat, which marked a new phase in her spiritual life. Some of these resolutions appear here:

"I resolve to do everything for Jesus; every work of mine, every trouble, I offer all to Jesus.

"I resolve that in order to serve God I no longer want to go to the movies if I do not know in advance whether they can be seen or not, if they are modest and not scandalous and immoral.

"I prefer to die rather than commit a mortal sin.

"*To say a Hail Mary daily so that the Lord may give me a happy death.* (Emphasis added)

"To obey [my teacher] and study even though I don't want to, for the love of Jesus."

Gianna's life from thenceforward became one of outstanding achievement and commitment. Her renewed application to her studies resulted in very good grades, the fruit of constant self-sacrifice on

9

her part, and her prayer life deepened. One of her teachers, Sr. Anna Rabbia, writes of her impressions of Gianna at that time: "The sweetness of her face, the gracefulness of her bearing, the smile on her lips were rays of the beauty of her soul, a reflection of her noble and pure heart. . . . Brought up in a deeply religious family, she had. . . learnt a deep piety. . . that serious and true piety which is the most beautiful ornament of a Christian young lady. . . . Diligent and committed to her studies, she was a model of respect and discipline." And this was a teenager who, shortly before this, could barely pass each school year!

Nevertheless, Gianna's energetic nature continued to manifest an exuberant joy in living. Her passions were mountain climbing and skiing. She declared that nowhere did she feel closer to God than at the summit of a great mountain covered with snow. This love of outdoor activity, not surprising considering the very picturesque mountain scenery surrounding the northern Italian home of her youth, was always a marked feature of her life.

Gianna was also artistic; she was a talented painter, and some of her Madonnas and scenic works are still treasured by her loved ones. The Beretta home often vibrated with the sound of her piano playing as well. She enjoyed the theater, the opera, and concerts. While always careful to dress modestly, she liked nice clothes; one of her friends remembers borrowing her beautiful ski jackets. Gianna's opinion was that a simple elegance is becoming to a Christian lady. She would have been the first to agree with the old adage that "a sad saint is a sorry saint."

The joy of Gianna

In Catholic Action

When she was twelve years old, Gianna, like other members of her family, became involved in Catholic Action in Genoa. Catholic Action was a movement whose aim was to mobilize the Catholic laity to live a more intense spiritual life, which in turn inspired many and varied types of charitable and apostolic work on every level of society.

The mission of Catholic Action can be seen in the challenging words often addressed to the movement by the Popes, especially by Pope Pius XII during the years in which Gianna was a member. "Oh, the good works which await you!" he exclaimed. "To reconstruct society on a Christian foundation; to renew men's esteem for the Gospel and its morals; to renew the family, restoring the crown of sacramental dignity to matrimony, giving back to spouses the sense of their obligations and the consciousness of their responsibility; to reaffirm at all levels of society the true understanding of authority, of discipline, of respect for the social order, of reciprocal rights and duties of the human person: this is your tomorrow. And to do this, you will need prayer, good example, ever-ready charity, helpfulness toward the humble and the afflicted, the perfect accomplishment of your duties in the family, at work, in society."

The program assigned to the young women was one which Gianna took to heart and lived to the full: *Eucharistic devotion, apostolic action, heroic purity.*

In this atmosphere, Gianna's good resolutions strengthened and matured. During the sad days of the Second World War, while she was

11

attending the University, Gianna became a leader in Catholic Action. All of the free time left over after her studies was devoted to apostolic work. She planned conferences, retreats and excursions for the younger girls, even putting her family's summer home at their disposal. The wartime travel conditions, food rations and the continual threat of bombing rendered this work very difficult. But Gianna persevered and worked untiringly for the good of souls who, more than ever in times like those, needed spiritual strength. Many testify that through Gianna's example, they rediscovered their faith in God.

Her words reflect how much she had internalized what she had learned in Catholic Action. "Do not be afraid to defend the honor of God, to defend the Church, the Pope and priests. This is the moment to act. We must not remain indifferent in the face of the enemy's campaign against religion and morals. We of Catholic Action must be the first to defend the sound foundation and the sacred Christian tradition of our homeland. . . . Would you be willing to give your lives for Christ the King? You who cannot say 'no' to your eyes, to your gluttony, you who find it difficult to help around the house or to pray for a few minutes. . .?"

In 1954, when St. Maria Goretti was canonized, Gianna drew this prophetic lesson for her young disciples: "Maria Goretti teaches us that life is beautiful when it is offered for the realization of great ideals, and to do this, we must be ready to give our lives." On another occasion, speaking to the young girls about purity, she said, "Purity presides over the just and licit use of sensible pleasures. Our body is sacred. Our body, joined to our soul, is an instrument for doing good. Purity is a virtue resulting from other virtues which lead to the preservation of purity. How are we to preserve our purity? We must surround our bodies with the hedge of sacrifice. Purity becomes beauty. Purity becomes strength. The one who is able to struggle and to stand firm is free."

Taking some of her young companions with her, she visited the abandoned poor and sick in their homes, bringing food and medicines and attending to the housecleaning. Once, upon returning from such a visit, she met a friend and explained that she needed to go home quickly to shower: "Please don't keep me long; I've just bathed an old woman and I'm covered with fleas!"

Gianna lived the golden years of her youth and young adulthood in the service of Catholic Action. The young girls were attracted by her shining example of self-sacrifice and prayer; they eagerly sought her advice and followed her counsels. Gianna was frequently elected to positions of leadership and trust in Catholic Action. In the last three years before her marriage, from 1952 to 1955, she was both president and delegate of her whole area. In this photo we see her leading a group of children on vacation in 1946.

A Time of Suffering

During the Second World War, Gianna's family moved back from Genoa to Bergamo, believing the latter to be safer from attack. The move was also motivated by concern for the failing health of Mr. Beretta. Gianna finished high school in Genoa and then returned to Bergamo to join her family.

In 1942, when she was 20, her beloved mother died at the age of fifty-five. The family had not yet recovered from this great sorrow when, only four and a half months later, her dear father followed his wife. This was a cause of great grief to Gianna, who loved her whole family tenderly.

Following these events, the Beretta children returned to their original home in Magenta, and Gianna began her medical studies at the University of Milan. Because of the war going on, these studies were, at times, interrupted. Later, Gianna transferred to the University of Pavia, where, finally, in 1949, she received her degree. She was eager and ready to place herself at the service of her brothers and sisters in need. Her mission was about to begin.

Gianna's Mission as a Doctor

Gianna now joined her brother Ferdinando as a doctor in Mesero, not far from Magenta. The people, who already knew her good family, flocked to her office with great confidence.

Gianna regarded her profession primarily as a service, not only to the bodies but also to the souls of those whom she attended. If a patient was too poor to afford medical help, Gianna assisted him free of charge. Her own words reveal her attitude towards her work, which she also carried out in the spirit of Catholic Action:

"Everyone in the world works, in some way, in the service of others. We doctors work directly on the person. The object of our knowledge and our work is the person before us who tells us about himself and says to us, 'Help me!'. . . We have opportunities that priests do not have. Our mission is not finished when medicines no longer help. There is the soul to lead towards God. Jesus is there, saying, 'Whoever visits the sick helps Me!' A priestly mission! Just as the priest may touch Jesus, so, too, we doctors touch Jesus in the bodies of our patients: the poor, the young, the old, children. May Jesus show Himself among us. May He find many doctors who offer themselves to Him. 'When you have finished your earthly profession. . . come to enjoy the life of God, because I was sick and you healed Me.'"

Dr. Gianna was noted for her special love for mothers and children. She went on to specialize in pediatrics in order to be able to help them more effectively.

It was also said of her:

"To be a doctor was a mission for Gianna. She gave herself to it unconditionally. . . . She set apart the mornings to visit her clients in their homes in the countryside. . . or in the hospital at Magenta. In the afternoons from 4:00 p.m. to 7:00 p.m. she was in her consulting rooms in Mesero." Another acquaintance informs us that Gianna did not leave the clinic until she had seen the last patient, no matter how long it took, so that sometimes she did not return home until 9 p.m.

Gianna's nurse-assistant, Luigia Galli Garavaglia, recalls that Gianna always went promptly to visit the sick who called her at night. "I remember that once she was called three times during the same night. She continued her assistance to the sick till the last day before entering the clinic for the birth of her last child. If the patient was poor, besides a free examination, Gianna gave him medicines and money."

For twelve years, this service formed a large part of Gianna's apostolate to those in need. Even after her marriage she continued her daily visits to the sick and her work at the clinic. One of her former schoolmates was not surprised that Gianna chose this profession because she had "felt sure that Gianna would choose something that would lead her to give herself to her neighbor, because from that time [her childhood] her thoughts were always turned to the poor, to the disowned and the sick."

Her Love for Life

Stories of Gianna's love for life abound. A man in Mesero one day confided to her his anguish at the birth of his handicapped child. Gianna understood his pain, calmed him and helped him to take steps to save the life of the child.

Another time a man came to Gianna to request an abortifacient for his wife. Gianna exclaimed bitterly: "You're coming to *me* to ask for it?" and quickly sent him on his way.

A young girl of the area called for medical help one day since she was suffering from severe abdominal cramps. Though she denied having done anything wrong, Gianna and her brother, who accompanied her, quickly realized that the girl, an unwed mother, had aborted her baby. Gianna was horrified and urged the girl repeatedly to repent and go to Confession. She asked parish priests to preach against this unspeakable crime. Her parish priest wrote: "She came to me to report with great sorrow the case of a young girl who wanted to abort. The tone of her voice, more than her words, expressed suffering and horror; she begged me to intervene, admonishing and exhorting the young woman to dread such a crime."

An older working woman who was facing an unexpected pregnancy and feared people's comments confided her embarrassment to Gianna. Gianna reassured her: "Isn't that a joy and pride? In this case we should not bother about what people say."

Her biographer, Fr. Fernando da Riese Pio X, attests that "Dr. Gianna was like a sister to expectant mothers, to encourage them to fulfill the creative plan of God. She did not leave them alone, with their doubts, anxieties, difficulties, temptations. . . . She placed herself near them as a sentinel defending life; she remained near them to welcome life, from the very beginning, as a life already in action, wanted, awaited, desired." Notes which she kept from a conference she attended sum up her thoughts on the sacredness of all life, even in cases in which the mother is endangered: "The doctor should not meddle. The right of the child to live is equal to the right of the mother's life. The doctor cannot decide; it is a sin to kill in the womb."

Gianna esteemed every life as a direct gift from the hands of God. She would not only preach this attitude with her words, but would eventually be called upon to live it with all its consequences. She was equal to the trial.

The Question of Vocation

The years sped by as Gianna devoted herself to her patients. Meanwhile, her older brother, now a priest, had gone to Brazil as a missionary. Gianna longed to join him and work at his side as a lay missionary, offering her medical services which were badly needed there. However, obstacle after obstacle prevented her from carrying out her wish. The necessary permissions were slow in coming. Gianna could not find anyone to replace her at the clinic in Mesero. Her spiritual director advised her to wait.

Gianna also came to the realization that her health was not sufficient for her to endure the rigors of the Brazilian climate. But what was she to do? A period of intense inner searching and suffering began.

In carrying out her medical practice, she several times encountered another leader in Catholic Action, the engineer Pietro Molla. She was struck by his apostolic spirit and he by her gentle charity and fearless practice of her faith. They met several times before Gianna began to realize that Pietro was in love with her.

She wrote to her brother, "As I informed you in my last letter, that engineer Molla. . . came, and if I were to tell you what I think of it, I would not know what to tell you now. . . .Pray for me, that I may do what God really wants from me."

In June 1954, the Marian Year, Gianna accompanied a pilgrimage of sick persons to Lourdes. She went with a great petition in her heart, as she herself relates: "I went to Lourdes to ask Our Lady what to do: go to the missions or marry? I reached home. . . and Pietro came in!"

That winter Pietro and Gianna spent more and more time together. On February 20th, 1955, Gianna accepted Pietro's proposal of marriage.

Pietro recalls in his memoir* addressed to Gianna: "That radiant summer of our engagement you were for me, more and more each day, the wonderful person who gave me the gift of her love for life, for climbing peaks and rushing down snowy slopes, the gift of joy at the enchantment of creation and of her ineffable smile, joy for the new family we would soon start, the joy of the grace of God."

On her part, Gianna rejoiced in God's gift to her and wrote Pietro many loving letters, speaking of their intention to "do all we can to make our new family a little Cenacle where Jesus reigns over all our affections, desires and actions. . . . We will become God's collaborators in creation. . . . Will I be the kind of wife and mother you have always hoped for? I want to be, because you deserve it and because I love you so much!"

"I love you so much, dearest Pietro, and every morning at Mass I offer my work and yours, my joys and sufferings and yours. Then I repeat the offering all day until evening. Good-bye and big, big kisses."

As Gianna shopped for the wedding dress fabric, she confided to her sister: "Do you know, I want to choose a very beautiful fabric because later on I want to make a chasuble out of it, for the first Mass of any one of my sons who may become a priest."

In September, 1955, Pietro and Gianna were married by Gianna's brother, Fr. Giuseppe. Pietro later described the surprise of the couple as the Mass began: "So many times my mind goes back to that sudden thunder of applause in the basilica of Magenta: it broke out when you stepped into the church and did not abate until you reached our wedding altar!" The good people of the place thus showed their deep affection and appreciation for Gianna and their joy at her happiness. Gianna walked down the long, carpeted aisle and "turned her big, wide-open black eyes this way and that, surprised at the clapping. . . ."

---

*After her death, Pietro wrote down his recollections of her in the form of a touching letter addressed to Gianna.

Gianna was thirty-three years old. She had found her "mission territory" as the wife and mother of a Christian family. She embarked on this new adventure with all her usual zest and joy in living, dreaming of the numerous and holy family which she hoped God would send her.

Gianna as a bride

*The photo at the beginning of this chapter
shows Gianna and Pietro during their engagement*

Wife and Mother

Gianna and Pietro took an extended honeymoon to Rome and all over Italy and Europe. Pietro wrote in a letter a few weeks after the wedding: "Her holy virtues, the gentle goodness and affection of Gianna, all her cares, give me the full joy and serenity which I asked of Jesus on my wedding day. With Gianna I am sure of forming a truly Christian family on which she will know how to draw the most beautiful heavenly graces. . . . We have begun and will continue with perseverance the daily recitation of the Rosary. May our Heavenly Mother always watch over us and give us the grace to be cheered by little angels," by which he meant the happy and healthy children he and Gianna hoped to have.

The couple settled down in a little house near the large firm where Pietro worked. The following year, in answer to their fervent prayers, their first child was born, a son, Pierluigi. Later came Mariolina in 1957, and Lauretta in 1959.

Gianna's pregnancies, which were a cause of great joy to her, were always difficult. Therefore, added to her natural maternal tenderness was an even greater affection for each child whom she had borne at risk to herself. Her husband wrote later: "In every pregnancy, how much prayer, how much confidence in Providence, how much strength in suffering! What a hymn of thanksgiving you raised to the Lord at each birth! For each of our children, you wished that, as soon as the Baptismal ceremony was over, every one of our children should be consecrated and entrusted to the special protection of Our Lady of Good Counsel.

". . .You continued to possess your joy of living, to enjoy the enchantment of creation, the mountains and their snow, concerts and the theater, as you had in your youth and during our engagement. . . . At home you were always busy; I cannot remember you doing nothing or even resting during the day, unless you were ill. Even with all the work our family gave you, you chose to persevere with your mission as a doctor in Mesero. . . . Your intentions, your actions were always fully consistent with your faith, with the apostolic, charitable spirit you had lived in your youth. . . ."

Pietro's work often took him on long journeys away from Gianna and the children. This was a cause of suffering to Gianna, because she loved her husband dearly. Many letters of hers attest to this deep affection. She worried that some accident would befall Pietro while he was away, especially when he had to fly. She kept him informed of every new accomplishment of the children, so that he would not miss any detail of their growing up. Often she referred to their little ones as "our treasures" or "our angels." Here are some excerpts from these charming letters:

"What a dear little angel our Pierluigi is! Daily he grows more beautiful, more lively, and seems to understand when we speak to him. . . . It is already three hours since our little children have fallen asleep like two little angels, tired with running and capering in the vineyard. . . . They keep me very busy and on my toes. . . . When the postman comes, Gigetto [Pierluigi] runs to see if papa has written. . . . They are at the age when they are a lot of work but they are magnificent with their innocent expressions. . . . They are always very lively and it is fortunate that they have guardian angels; they are into mischief constantly. . . . Pierluigi always recites a Hail Mary for his Dad and ends by saying, 'Papa, come back soon.' Mariolina joins her little hands and sends kisses to Our Lady. What treasures they are!"

When her third child was born, the older children were sent to stay with a friend in another village for a few days. Gianna wrote, "They phone me every day and are very happy to learn of their new sister (Pierluigi calls her that). Furthermore, last night he wanted me to send her to the phone: 'I want to speak to my little sister.'. . . He has already said that he will not hit the new baby but the old one. . . 'yes.'"

Gianna's sister Virginia tells us that when the children began to come, Gianna had to give up her daily Mass and Communion: "Only during the last years of her life, the time of the only Mass celebrated in the little church. . . coincided with the time when she had to get the children ready to go to the nursery school and give them breakfast. It was no longer possible for her, to her great sorrow, to receive Communion daily and to assist at the celebration of the Eucharistic sacrifice." Her husband, in America for work-related travel at the time, could continue to attend daily Mass. Gianna wrote him, "How many prayers for your family! You always find time to hear and follow Holy Mass. Unfortunately, I can never move. This morning, Mariolina was already awake at 5 o'clock and at 6 I had to get up, dress her and take her to the hall to make her play; otherwise she would have awakened Pierluigi with her shrill voice."

One of Gianna's friends still remembers a visit from the happy mother with her children: "In 1961 [this was the year before Gianna's death], Gianna came to see me with her children. The children were talking, singing and enjoying themselves. She watched them in silence, and every now and then, she arranged the dress of one, caressed the hair of the other and looked attentively at them. One could see that she was satisfied and proud of them." Her husband echoed this observation: "Gianna enjoyed her children, lived for them and was so proud of them. She was so happy." And Gianna herself wrote: "I am always happy with Pietro, with our three magnificent children, and I thank God much for it. I would so like to have another child."

The Last Months

Gianna and Pietro already had three beautiful children, but they were anxious to have more. To their great sorrow, Gianna had two miscarriages. The couple redoubled their prayers.

Pietro wrote, "In every circumstance, you always referred to and entrusted yourself to the Lord's will. Every day, I remember, you prayed and you meditated; you had your conversation with God and you thanked Him for the ineffable gift of our wonderful children. And you were very happy.

"You greatly desired another child; you prayed and you asked others to pray the Lord to grant you this wish. And so He did, but that divine favor would cost you your life."

In the fall of 1961, Gianna became aware that she was expecting again, but difficulties accompanied the joyous news. It was discovered that a painful ovarian cyst was causing the problem. As Gianna, being a doctor, well knew, the only sure hope for saving her life was to remove the uterus, causing the death of her unborn child. The other option was to surgically remove the growth, letting the pregnancy continue, endangering both mother and child, but holding out some hope for the child.

Years before, while still in Catholic Action, Gianna had been present at a conference given by Msgr. Luigi Crespi on the subject of "Matrimony and the Consequent Duties of a Christian Mother." The priest explained to the young women that "when the mother and child are in danger, preference should be given to the life of the child."

Gianna had later taught this principle to the other young girls. Now she found herself faced with this very dilemma.

Gianna did not even think twice: she chose the surgery which left hope for her unborn child while seriously endangering her own life. She said, "With faith and hope I am trusting in the Lord even against science's terrible sentence. I trust in God, but now it is up to me to fulfill my duty as a mother. I renew the offering of my life to the Lord. I am ready for anything as long as my baby is saved."

The surgeon, deeply moved at her decision, said to Gianna's brothers at the hospital, "Behold the Catholic mother!" The doctors later confessed that they hoped that Gianna would spontaneously miscarry so that they could then remove the diseased uterus and save her life. But such was not to be.

The surgery seemed to go well. Gianna rejoiced that her baby was safe. The long, anxious months went by. . . the most dangerous point, the fifth month, passed without event. . . Gianna's hopes rose. Perhaps the Lord would hear her prayers and spare her for the sake of her husband and small children. In fact, about a month before the baby's birth, Gianna asked Pietro to bring her some fashion magazines from Paris. She examined them and made plans to make over her wardrobe after the happy event.

Yet she felt her time was short. Let us allow Pietro to tell us the rest of the touching story in his own words:

> *During those long months, you never said a word to me about your keen awareness, as a physician, of what lay in store for you. Unquestionably, you did so out of the desire to spare me the pain.*
>
> *Many times you asked me to forgive you for causing me worry. You told me that, more than ever, you needed tender love and understanding.*
>
> *I was indeed worried about your quiet tidying up, for days on end, every corner of our house, every drawer, every clothing item, every personal belonging, as if you were about to depart on a very long journey. But I never dared ask myself, or you, why.*
>
> *Just a few days before the delivery, with a firm yet serene tone, with a penetrating gaze I have never forgotten, you told me: "If you have to make a decision between me and the child, do not hesitate: choose the child—I demand it—save him."*

From that moment on, I feared and suffered with you.

On Holy Saturday morning we had the wondrous joy and the divine gift of the baby we had been expecting: Gianna Emanuela.

After a few hours, your suffering started; the pain was excruciating, overwhelming, and it made you constantly invoke your mother, who was already in heaven. You knew you were dying and you felt the wrenching anguish of leaving all our children in their tender years; yet you never told me.

When you held our infant daughter in your arms, you gave her a deeply loving look, a gaze that betrayed the inexpressible grief that came from knowing you would not be able to nurture her and soon you would not see her any more.

But even then, you never said anything to me about your fear, much less about your certainty that you would soon die. Only to Sr. Maria Eugenia Crippa, who worked in the obstetrics ward at the Monza hospital, did you say when you were admitted there: "Sister, I have come here to die this time." And you said it—as Sr. Maria Eugenia remembers—"with a look of grief for the life you knew you were leaving, yet with serenity. A true model of a heroic mother."

I remember when you told me, on Wednesday morning, with a serenity so sublime as to be otherworldly: "Pietro, I am healed now. Pietro, I was on the other side already and if only you knew what I saw. Someday I'll tell you. But since we were too happy, our life was too good, with our wonderful children, full of health and grace, with all of Heaven's blessings, they sent me back here to suffer some more, because it is not right to reach the Lord's presence without having suffered a great deal." This was and still is for me your testament of joy and suffering.

Then the pain intensified again.

You asked to receive Jesus in the Eucharist, at least on your lips, even Thursday and Friday, when you could not swallow the Sacred Host any more. A godly priest, Father Olinto Marella, was by your side, too.

The Lord could not, did not accede to my weeping, my supplications, my vows as I served, always barely holding back my tears, Father Marella's Mass in the hospital's church. He could not accede to the prayers offered by our children, by that godly priest, by our near and dear ones, and by all the many, many people who were in trepidation for your life, as if you were a member of their own families.

As you suffered on your death bed, you repeated many times: "Jesus, I love You, Jesus, I love You!"

. . . You finally came home on Saturday morning, your life nearly at its end. Maybe you heard the voices of our children as they were waking up in the next room. Almost at the same time, you rose to Heaven and took your place among God's saints.

Just a few hours after Gianna was brought home from the hospital, she died. It was eight o'clock in the morning, the Saturday after Easter, April 28, 1962.

We all know that we tend to take very much for granted those with whom we live on a day-to-day basis. If Pietro could write thus of his wife with whom he had lived six and a half years, it should tell us something about Gianna and her virtue.

*From left to right: Mariolina, Pierluigi,
Gianna Emanuela, and Laura at Courmayeur
where the family often vacationed. This photo
was taken the year after their mother's death.*

After Her Death

The day after Gianna's death, the child for whom she gave her life was baptized. Gianna had wished to name the little girl Emanuela, meaning "God is with us." Pietro prefaced this name with that of his beloved wife, and thus she was named Gianna Emanuela.

Gianna's sisters lovingly helped Pietro (who still lives in Magenta) to raise the children. The oldest daughter Mariolina joined her mother in heaven two years after Gianna's death. Pierluigi, as an adult, went into business and married. Laura studied economics.

And what became of the little Giannina?

In October 1997, in Rio de Janeiro, Brazil, Pope John Paul II sat listening to various speakers for the Second World Day of the Family. As the talks progressed, a young woman stepped forward and offered her testimony. At the end she prayed:

"Thank you, Mother. Thank you for having given me life twice: in conception and when you permitted me to be born, deciding for my life. Intercede so that all mothers and families may always come to you with confidence."

It was Gianna Emanuela. As he heard these moving words, the Pope wept.

This young woman is a medical doctor today, like her mother. She cares for Alzheimer's patients and lives with her father in Mesero.

It was not the first time that the Pope met the younger Gianna. On April 24, 1994, Pope John Paul II proclaimed Gianna Beretta Molla

"Blessed." Present at the ceremony were her husband, surviving children, and four of her brothers and sisters!

The Pope said of her:

> [Blessed Gianna] had the grace of a united family, rich in faith and love. She was a happy mother, but a great trial touched her in the course of her fourth pregnancy. In the dramatic choice between saving her life and that of her child which she carried in her womb, she did not hesitate to sacrifice herself. What a heroic witness is hers, a true hymn to life, in violent contrast with a certain mentality pervasive today! May her sacrifice infuse courage in as many as participate. . . in the movement for life and in other similar organizations in order that the intangible dignity of every human existence be recognized, from the moment of conception up to natural decline, as a primary and fundamental value in respect to every other human and social right.

May Blessed Gianna intercede for all of us who must live in the culture of death, especially for all the mothers who are tempted by fear or selfishness to destroy the lives of their unborn children. May she give us her powerful aid from Heaven to build the culture of life.

Special thanks to Bl. Gianna's husband, Pietro Molla, and to the Blessed Gianna Beretta Molla Society. For holy cards, novena prayers, or to report favors received, please contact:

Blessed Gianna Beretta Molla Society
P.O. Box 59557
Philadelphia, PA 19102-9557
www.gianna.org

"Mamma's house of gold" (see Prologue). Here we see Gianna's burial place, to the right, outlined in gold. In the mosaic, Gianna is offering her daughter to Our Lady of Lourdes, assisted by Teresina, Pietro's young sister, who had died years earlier.

Prayer from the Votive Mass of Blessed Gianna

Grant, O Father, that Your faithful
following the example of Blessed Gianna
may faithfully live the grace
which consecrates spousal love and family affection
and with grateful hearts
may welcome children
in whom the image of Christ shines
surrounding them with vigilant love
from the first moments of their lives.
Through our Lord and our God
who lives and reigns with You
in the unity of the Holy Spirit,
forever and ever. Amen.

The Pope greets Gianna Emanuela

L'Osservatore Romano

Gianna Emanuela, Laura and Mr. Molla present gifts to the Holy Father during the Beatification Mass

L'Osservatore Romano

Mr. Molla receives Communion from the Holy Father

Gianna Emanuela receives Communion from the Holy Father

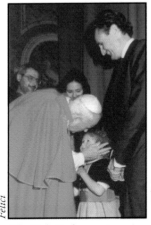

The Holy Father greets Pierluigi and his family

The living brothers and sisters of Gianna who were present at the beatification. Left to right: Msgr. Giuseppe, Mother Virginia, Fr. Alberto, Zita

Blessed Gianna enjoying her children

St. Martin de Porres Lay Dominican Community
3050 Gap Knob Road
New Hope, KY 40052
270-325-3061